D1395088

Ron and Joyce Cave, both senior officials of the
Cambridgeshire Educational Authority,
have written and developed these
books to be read by children on their own.

A simple question is asked about each topic discussed
and is then immediately answered.

A second, more general question follows which is
designed to provoke further thinking by the child
and may require parental assistance.

The answers to these second questions
are found at the end of the book.

Designed and produced by
Aladdin Books Ltd
70 Old Compton Street · London W1
for: The Archon Press Ltd
8 Butter Market · Ipswich

Published in the U.S.A. 1982 by
Gloucester Press
730 Fifth Avenue · New York NY 10019
All rights reserved

Library of Congress Catalog
Card No: 81-84534

ISBN 531 044203

WHAT ABOUT?
MOTORCYCLES

Ron and Joyce Cave

Illustrated by
David West and Peter Hutton

GLOUCESTER PRESS
New York · Toronto

Motorbikes

Motorbikes are fun to look at and
fun to ride. They provide a quick
and efficient way of getting around
in city traffic and they use less
gasoline than most cars. But they can
also be ridden over long distances,
on rough ground, and in lots of
different kinds of bike sports.
The picture below is of a Honda,
a popular modern bike. It shows
the main parts of a motorbike.

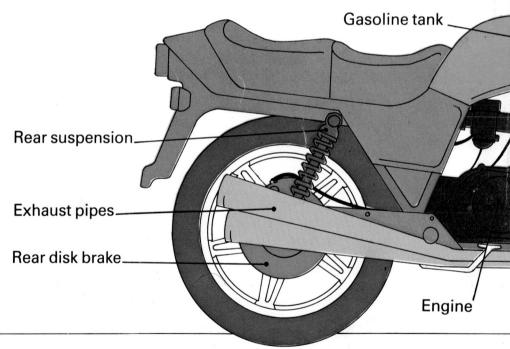

Gasoline tank

Rear suspension

Exhaust pipes

Rear disk brake

Engine

All bikes have the same basic parts but not all bikes look the same. They come in many different shapes and sizes. This book tells you about some of the colorful and exciting bikes you can see today. It shows you some of the earliest bikes ever invented, too, as well as trying to look into the future to guess what sort of bikes we might be riding in the year 2000!

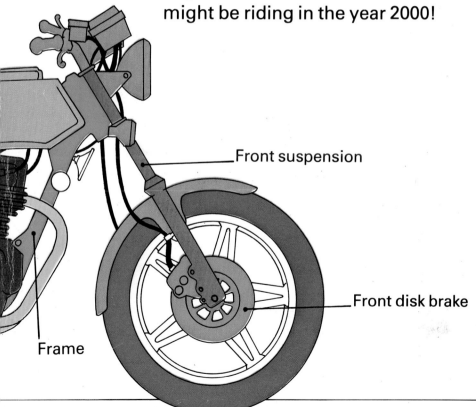

Front suspension

Front disk brake

Frame

Steam power

The first motorcycles were made by fitting steam engines to ordinary bicycles. They were hard to control and not very successful. The American Copeland steam-driven machine of 1885 was the world's first mass-produced motorcycle.
It had a steam engine which was mounted on the steering column.
The rider sat on a seat mounted above the large rear wheel. He must have needed a lot of courage to ride it!

Why were steam-powered motorcycles not very successful?

Although the Copeland steam engine weighed less than 200lbs, (91 kilos) most were much heavier and not very powerful. When the lighter, more efficient gasoline engine was invented, steam power could not compete.

What else was steam power used for?

Copeland 1885

Early Motorcycles

The first really practical motorcycle was driven by a gasoline engine. This lightweight bike, built in 1897, was the "Werner." It was designed in France by two brothers named Werner. It had a thin, light frame, narrow tires and a saddle like that of an ordinary bicycle. The engine was placed above the front wheel. It drove the front wheel by means of a twisted leather belt. Later the Werner brothers made another bike with the engine low down between the wheels.

Where do we put the engine today?

On today's motorbikes the engine is placed low down on the frame between the wheels. The position of the first Werner engine, over the front wheel, made the bike difficult to steer and top heavy. This meant that the bike was not very stable on wet roads and might fall over if it skidded.

What does "stable" mean?

Werner 1897

The Engine

Motorbike engines are either two-stroke or four-stroke. They are driven by a series of small explosions. Inside the engine air and gasoline are mixed and squeezed together. An electric spark from a spark plug makes the air and gasoline mixture explode. Hot gas from this explosion drives a piston up and down inside a tube called the cylinder. The power of the piston moving up and down is used to drive the back wheel.

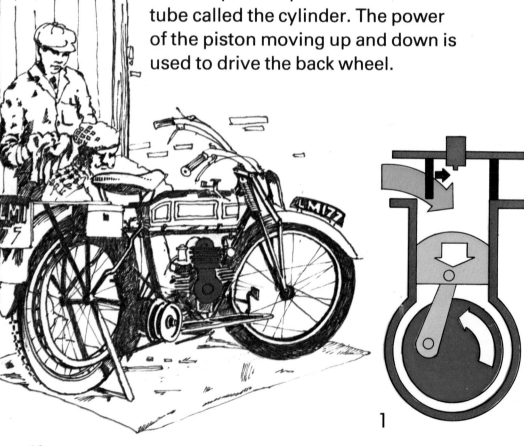

1

What is a four-stroke engine?

The picture shows how a four-stroke works. Gasoline and air are sucked in on the first stroke. On the second stroke the piston rises, squeezing this mixture, which the spark ignites. The resulting explosion pushes the piston down on the third stroke.

What happens on the fourth or exhaust stroke?

4-stroke engine

2

3

4

War years

In World War I (1914–18) motorbikes were used for many jobs which had been done by horses up to then. The bikes were easier to look after and less trouble to pull out of the mud. They could get from one part of the battlefield to another quickly, even over rough ground. They were used again in World War II (1939–45) in many different ways. This time they were used as real fighting machines. Sometimes both a motorbike and its sidecar carried machine guns.

What sorts of jobs did motorbikes do?

The picture shows a big Harley Davidson used by military police. Motorbikes were also used for carrying dispatches (messages). Some were fitted with sidecar stretchers to carry the wounded. Small, collapsible motorbikes were packed in big cans and dropped by parachute.

Why is this bike painted green?

Harley Davidson

Lightweight bikes

Many young people long for the day when they can own their first motorbike. Lightweight bikes are popular because they are cheap to buy and cheap to run. In the 1950s and 1960s mopeds (bikes with engines of no more than 49cc) and scooters were bought by a lot of people. Now the first machine bought is often a lightweight motorbike with a single cylinder engine. The Japanese were the first to make very large numbers of these bikes.

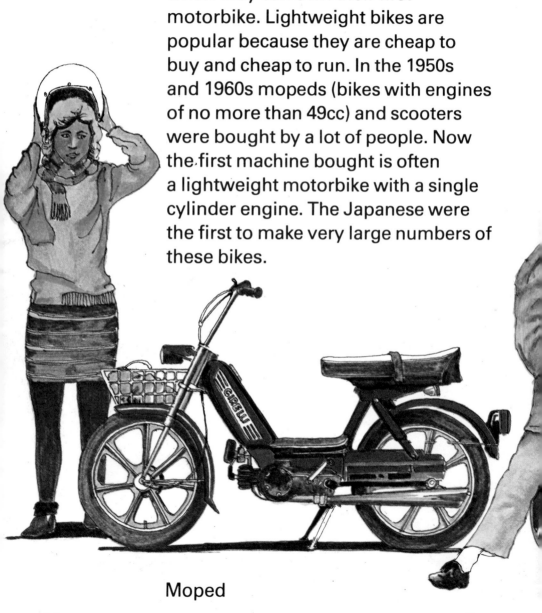

Moped

What is meant by "single cylinder"?

Engines are described by the number of cylinders they have and the space inside these cylinders. The space is measured in cubic centimeters (cc).

Can you now say what is meant by a 49cc engine?

Yamaha 125cc

Vespa 50cc

15

Superbikes

When a motorbike has an engine size of 750cc or over we class it as a superbike. These are the really big, powerful machines. "Near-racers" are superbikes that can be driven almost like true racing bikes. The bike shown in the picture is a near-racer. It is an Italian two-cylinder Ducati 900. Such a powerful bike needs plenty of stopping power. This Ducati has three disk brakes.

Ducati 900cc Sport Desmo

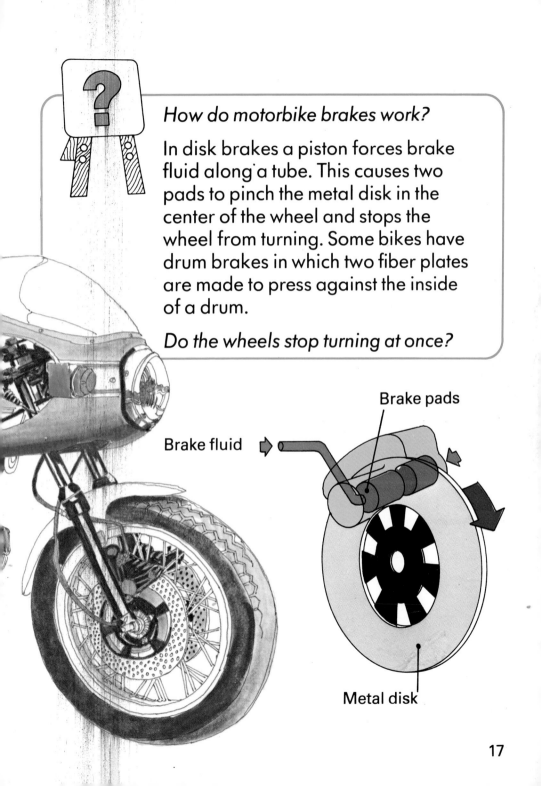

How do motorbike brakes work?

In disk brakes a piston forces brake fluid along a tube. This causes two pads to pinch the metal disk in the center of the wheel and stops the wheel from turning. Some bikes have drum brakes in which two fiber plates are made to press against the inside of a drum.

Do the wheels stop turning at once?

Brake pads

Brake fluid

Metal disk

Racing bikes

Road racing is a very popular motorbike sport. Different bike manufacturers have their own teams of riders. Every year there is a World Championship in which riders from all over Europe and America compete. Motorbike racing is very exciting to watch. The riders heel their machines over at steep angles as they speed round the bends. Sometimes the tires lose their grip. If the rider falls off his leather suit will help him slide across the track without injury.

What stops tires from losing their grip?

The treads (raised patterns) on a tire surface help it to grip on wet roads. They are also designed to help water run away quickly. "Slicks" are smooth tires without treads. They go faster over dry surfaces but they are used only for racing. They are illegal on the highway.

Why are treads safer on wet roads?

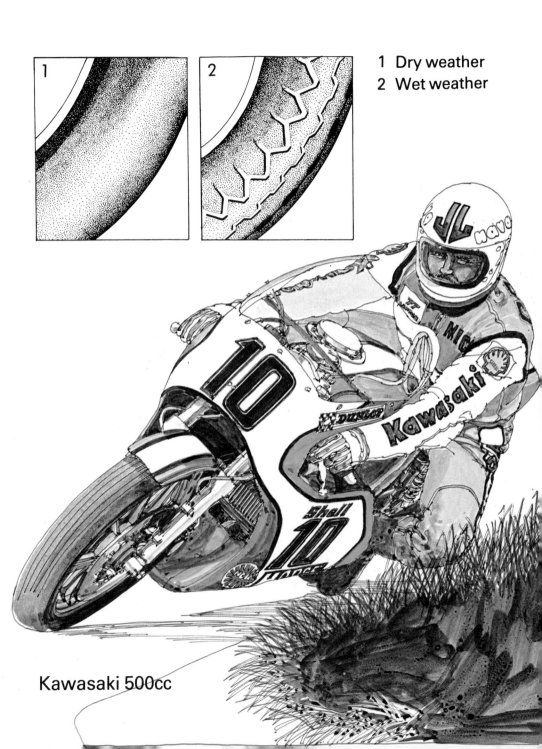

1 Dry weather
2 Wet weather

Kawasaki 500cc

Honda 400cc

Trials bikes

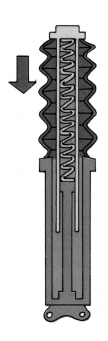

There are many different motorbike sports. Moto cross (or scrambling as it is sometimes called), hill climbing and trials riding are all good fun. In motorbike trials the riders test their skill and bike control over rough country. The idea is to keep going however difficult the course may be. Points are lost each time a rider stops or puts a foot on the ground. Trials bikes need very good suspension and big, chunky tires to grip in the mud.

What do we mean by good suspension?

The telescopic forks and rear shock absorbers make up the suspension of the bike. They both have steel springs which help to absorb bumps. A piston inside an oil-filled cylinder stops the springs themselves from bouncing too much.

What other parts of a motorbike help to give you a smooth ride?

Drag bikes

Road racers go much faster than ordinary bikes but drag racing machines are the fastest of all. The aim in drag racing is to cover the quarter of a mile course (402m) in the shortest time possible. The fastest drag bikes can do this in under eight seconds from a standing start. They travel at over 190mph (300kph), their riders almost lying over the machines.

What makes the bikes used for drag racing special?

Some of the biggest bikes have three engines totaling 3500cc. A special fuel is used and a very wide rear tire is fitted to improve the grip on the track.

What is a standing start?

Three-engined Honda Dragster

Indian chopper

Choppers

Some owners like their machines to look different from ordinary motorbikes. They change the appearance (this is called "customizing" the machine), usually by making the front forks longer. This gives the forks a greater "rake" or angle. The front wheel is often small. Sometimes a strange rear end is added with as many as four back wheels! Bikes like the Indian chopper in the picture have been changed so much that the only part of the original machine remaining is the engine.

Why are bikes like these called "choppers"?

To make a chopper many of the parts of an ordinary bike are cut or chopped away and new parts added. The frame and gasoline tank are painted and other parts are chrome plated.

What other types of vehicles are "customized"?

The Future

We can only guess about motorbikes
of the future but some of today's
bikes can give us a clue about what
they might look like. The amazing
machine in the picture is the "Booleroo."
It is designed for safety (with
improved brakes), efficiency and
comfort. Its streamlined body looks
good and it is practical too. Its
arrow shape is designed for speed but
it also contains space for luggage
and for the rider to sit inside in
comfort protected from the weather.

Booleroo

How can bikes be made safer and to run more cheaply?

Tires might be fitted which do not puncture. Brakes can be made to work better to prevent skidding in the rain. New fuels, cheaper than gasoline, may be discovered.

Do you have any ideas?

Answers

What else was steam power used for?

Before the invention of the gasoline engine steam power was used to power all forms of transport such as trucks, cars, ships and trains.

What does "stable" mean?

"Stable" means firm and steady.

What happens on the fourth or exhaust stroke?

The exhaust fumes are pushed out.

Why is this bike painted green?

Most military vehicles are painted in a color to blend with the landscape so that they cannot be easily seen.

Can you now say what is meant by a 49cc engine?

The engine has a cylinder capacity of 49 cubic centimeters.

Do the wheels stop turning at once?

In normal braking the brakes stop the wheels turning gradually. A skid is caused when the wheels lock or stop turning at once.

Why are treads safer on wet roads?

Tires with treads help to get rid of the rainwater and therefore help the bike to grip the road.

What other parts of a motorbike help to give you a smooth ride?

The tires and the saddle have a little give in them to help cushion the ride.

What is a standing start?

A drag bike must not be moving before the green starting light. If it does then it is disqualified.

What other types of vehicles are customized?

Cars, vans and trucks are popular vehicles to customize.

Index